DANGEROUS ANIMALS

James Nixon

W
FRANKLIN WATTS
LONDON•SYDNEY

Franklin Watts
338 Euston Road
London NW1 3BH

Franklin Watts Australia
Level 17/207 Kent Street
Sydney, NSW 2000

Series Editor: Amy Stephenson
Planning and production by Discovery Books Ltd
Editor: James Nixon
Series designer: D.R. ink
Picture researcher: James Nixon
Picture credits: Cover image: Shutterstock (Volodymyr Burdiak)
Alamy: pp. 7 bottom (Stock Connection Blue), 27 middle (WaterFrame). Corbis: pp. 5 top (Gallo Images/
Martin Harvey), 6 top (Minden Pictures/Pete Oxford), 8 top (Minden Pictures/Heidi & Hans-Juergen Koch), 9
top (Foto Natura/Minden Pictures/James Christensen), 10 top (All Canada Photos/Wayne Lynch), 11 bottom
(Foto Natura/Minden Pictures/James Christensen), 20 middle (Anup Shah), 21 top (Visuals Unlimited/Robert
Pickett), 23 top (All Canada Photos/Wayne Lynch), 24 top (Minden Pictures/Mike Parry), 25 bottom (Image
Source), 26 bottom (Tom Brakefield), 29 bottom (Steve Parish Publishing/Steve Parish). Getty Images: p. 4 (Hali
Sowle Images). Shutterstock: pp. 2 (Audrey Snider-Bell), 5 bottom (Jamen Percy), 6 bottom-left (Skynavin), 6
bottom-right (Brooke Whatnall), 7 top (Heiko Kiera), 9 middle (James van den Broek), 9 bottom (Audrey Snider-
Bell), 10 bottom (Rusty Dodson), 11 top (Dennis Donohue), 12 top (Shvak), 12 bottom (Michael Lynch), 13
middle-left (clearviewstock), 13 middle-right (reptiles4all), 13 bottom (Sergey Uryadnikov), 14 (dirkr), 15 top
(Trevor Kelly), 15 bottom (Heiko Kiera), 16 (Sergey Uryadnikov), 17 top (Four Oaks), 17 bottom (smileimage9),
18 (pinthong nakon), 19 top (Stephen), 19 middle (Scott E Read), 19 bottom (Galyna Andrushko), 20 top
(Ddniki), 20 bottom (J Reinieke), 21 bottom (Peter Schwarz), 22 (Critterbiz), 23 bottom (Anan Kaewkhammul),
25 top (Michael Bogner), 25 middle (Willyam Bradberry), 25 bottom (Kristina Vackova), 27 top (Krzysztof
Odziomek), 27 bottom (Cigdem Sean Cooper), 28 top-left (R Gino Santa Maria), 29 top-right (orlandin).

Dewey number 591.6'5
ISBN: 978 1 4451 3597 7

A CIP catalogue record for this book is available from the British Library.
Printed in China

Franklin Watts is a division of Hachette Children's Books,
an Hachette UK company.
www.hachette.co.uk

CONTENTS

All words in **bold** can be found in the glossary on page 31.

THE WORLD'S DEADLIEST CREATURES

WATCH OUT! It's a killer world out there. Some of the animals that roam our planet are deadly. There are large **predators** that might want to eat you alive. But many dangerous creatures are small and lurk out of sight. If people fail to spot them in time, tragedy strikes!

SKILLS THAT KILL

Some killer creatures can appear to be cute and harmless while others are as fierce and dangerous as they look. Different animals are deadly in their own unique ways. Terrifying snakes, scorpions and spiders kill their victims with lethal **venom**. Savage animals like big cats, sharks and crocodiles rip their prey to shreds with their powerful jaws. If you don't live in the same part of the world as these predators, count yourself lucky.

AMAZING FACT
Human attacks

Each year, over one million people are attacked and injured by animals in the wild. It is estimated that around 100,000 people are killed by these attacks.

MAN-EATER JOKE

Q How does the crocodile greet other animals?

A Pleased to eat you!

The saltwater crocodile is not a fussy eater. It will attack almost any animal, from leopards and pythons to kangaroos and humans!

A lion attacks a young antelope in south-west Africa.

WHY DO ANIMALS ATTACK?

Animals can get angry and attack for many reasons. They may be protecting their babies or **territory**. If they are very hungry they might fancy a tasty, human meal. Some animals are just aggressive by nature. Humans must be careful around wild animals. If animals feel threatened, the chances are they will attack.

AMAZING FACT
The fiercest creature

Wolverines are said to be the fiercest creatures on the planet. Despite its name the wolverine is not a wolf or a dog, but a weasel. Armed with powerful jaws and sharp claws they are amazingly strong for their size. A wolverine (below) is no bigger than a medium-sized pet dog, but it can kill prey as large as an adult deer and will attack grizzly and polar bears!

TRUE OR FALSE?

If you are bitten or stung by one of the most venomous creatures on the planet you will probably die. **True or False?**

FALSE! Medicines called **antivenoms** have been developed to treat the victims of venomous bites and stings. However, a person who has been **injected** with venom should get to a hospital, fast. An antivenom must be taken before it is too late.

KILLER SNAKES

Snakes are the deadliest venomous animals on Earth. They kill more people than any other type of animal that can inject venom.

A diamondback rattlesnake rattles its tail at rapid speed.

SNAKE-BITES

One of the scariest sounds in nature is the rattling scales on the tail of a diamondback rattlesnake. This is a warning that it is about to attack. You'd better run fast because these American rattlesnakes will lunge forward with their fangs, launching attacks that are so quick they are almost impossible to dodge. Beware – their fangs are long and their venom is deadly.

The death adder from Australia has the fastest snake-strike in the world. It can attack, inject venom and go back to its striking position in almost one tenth of a second!

Death adders do not go out hunting. They lie in wait for their prey.

AMAZING FACT
King cobra

The king cobra found in Asia is one of the most deadly snakes on the planet. Its venom is lethal and a bite will quickly leave its victim unable to breathe. A king cobra can grow to over five metres long, making it the longest of all venomous snakes. When it is angry it can make itself as tall as a fully grown man and look him in the eye.

TOXIC TERRORS

The African black mamba is one of the most feared snakes in the world. Its bite is five times more venomous than a king cobra's. In each mouthful it has enough venom to kill 40 people. The black mamba is also the fastest-moving snake. At top speed it can reach 20 kph (12 mph) and it can also climb trees.

The prize for the most **toxic** snake goes to the inland taipan from central Australia. The venom in its bite can kill a human in as little as 45 minutes.

Black mambas are fast, agile and very aggressive.

ALL WRAPPED UP

The world's largest snake is the green anaconda (right) from South America. These terrifying creatures can grow up to nine metres in length and weigh up to 200 kilograms. Anacondas are not venomous – instead they **coil** around their victims and squeeze them until they stop breathing. Once you are wrapped up there is no escape.

A man fights off a green anaconda, which is trying to wrap itself around his body.

TRUE OR FALSE?

An anaconda eats victims as large as deer – whole and head first. **True or False?**

TRUE! But it takes a while to **digest**. It may not need another meal for weeks or even months.

A large, female black widow with its bright red warning spot meets her male partner. Female black widows often eat the males shortly after **mating** with them.

SHOCKING SPIDERS

Spiders are among the most feared creatures on the planet, although most are completely harmless to humans. In some parts of the world a few of them are deadly.

BLACK WIDOWS

The black widow is the most famous of the scary spiders. It **preys** on small insects and other spiders but will also bite humans if threatened. When it bites a prey insect, it injects it with lethal venom. Once the prey is dead, the black widow injects it with digestive juices from its fangs. These juices turn it to mush, which the spider then sucks up. The female black widow is much larger and more dangerous to humans than the male. Although she won't turn you to mush if she bites you, her venom can be lethal.

TRUE OR FALSE?

The black widow spider's venom is 15 times more powerful than a rattlesnake's. **True or False?**

TRUE! For females at least, who are three times more venomous than the males.

HIDDEN DANGERS

The Brazilian wandering spider is one of the most aggressive and venomous spiders in the world. This large, brown hairy spider prowls the **rainforest** floor searching for prey. It also hides in dark places under logs and in houses and cars. If disturbed by humans, it will attack. Be careful when you open your lunchbox. These spiders have been found in crates of bananas transported across the world! In 2013 a six-year-old girl from Alaska, USA, went running and screaming to her mother when she found a wandering spider hiding in the fruit bowl!

A Brazilian wandering spider finds a blue frog to eat on the rainforest floor.

AMAZING FACT
Bird-eating spiders

The Goliath birdeater (below) from South America is the largest **tarantula** and a terrifying sight. It is the size of a human head and has fangs as long as cat's claws. These giant beasts lunge forward with venomous attacks in the blink of an eye, and can eat prey as large as birds. If the tarantula feels threatened, it will kick hairs off its body. The hairs are itchy and if they get into your eyes or throat they can be harmful.

The funnel web spider (above) from Australia is particularly nasty and dangerous. Funnel webs live near to humans and will wander into gardens, garages and even swimming pools. Attacks are vicious and venomous. The spider grips tightly to its victim's skin and bites many times. Some funnel web spiders have fangs that are sharp enough to bite through shoes and fingernails!

TOXIC SCORPIONS

Scorpions are **arachnids** like spiders, which means they have eight legs. They also have pincers at the front to grab their victims and a curved stinging tail at the back. These venomous stingers kill up to 5,000 humans every year.

This close-up of a scorpion tail shows venom dripping from its tip.

AMAZING FACT
A clever stinger

A scorpion holds a supply of venom in its tail. If the venom runs out it can be days before the scorpion can produce more. To stop this from happening, scorpions choose how much venom they inject each time they make an attack. A scorpion will save up its biggest doses for larger threats, such as humans.

SCORPION INVASION

Scorpions are so dangerous because they turn up in people's homes. Stepping on one can be deadly. Arizona bark scorpions in the United States **hibernate** in groups in houses where they climb walls and hang upside down off the ceilings. They only grow to eight centimetres in length but a small dose of their venom is highly toxic.

SCORPION JOKE

Q What's the best thing about deadly scorpions?

A They've got poisonality!

Arizona bark scorpion

Most scorpion deaths happen in busy, crowded parts of Mexico and Brazil. The Brazilian yellow scorpion is happy to live in the city and kills many small children whose bodies are more vulnerable to the scorpion's venom.

STINGERS IN THE DESERT

The deathstalker (right) is the most toxic scorpion on the planet. Just a small sting is agony and the chances of survival are slim. Luckily, this terrifying creature lives away from most humans in the deserts of the Middle East and North Africa.

Another danger that lurks in the African desert is the fat-tailed scorpion. This mean-looking predator has a large and vicious curling tail. The sting at the end contains a powerful mixture of venom that could easily kill a human. Even from a distance you are not safe. It can flick the lethal fluid from its tail into the eyes of its victims.

TRUE OR FALSE?

The deathstalker's lethal venom could be developed as medicine for humans. **True or False?**

TRUE! It has been discovered that a part of its venom could be helpful in treating diseases such as **cancer**. So deathstalkers are not all bad!

A fat-tailed scorpion feasts on a cricket, but its venom is even strong enough to kill a human.

FROGS, BATS AND LIZARDS

So what is the most toxic animal in the world? Is it a snake? A spider? A scorpion? In fact it is a tiny and extremely colourful frog that lives deep in the rainforest in South America.

Poison dart frogs come in many different colours, from neon green to electric blue (left). These colours are a warning to other animals that they are highly dangerous. These frogs have skin that is covered with the world's most lethal animal poison. Just by touching a frog, the poison can seep into your **bloodstream** and cause your heart to fail. The golden poison dart frog is the most toxic. One frog contains enough poison to kill 20 people or an army of 10,000 mice!

BLOODSUCKING BATS

Another frightening creature found in South America is the spooky vampire bat. They live in huge colonies up to 5,000 strong. With their sharp teeth they bite into the victim's skin and suck blood for up to 20 minutes at a time. They come out at night, searching for animals to prey on. Special heat sensors in their

AMAZING FACT
Deadly darts

Poison dart frogs get their name from the weapons used by rainforest people. Local hunters catch the frogs and rub the tips of their arrows and darts on the frogs' backs to collect the poison. The poison is so lethal that when the arrows are fired at an animal it will die within minutes.

A vampire bat bares its fangs.

nose guide them to a part of their prey that is full of blood and best to feed on. Vampire bats don't kill their prey with their bloodsucking attacks, but they can **infect** their victims with deadly diseases such as **rabies**.

LARGE LIZARDS

Most lizards are harmless but there are a few that are truly terrifying. The world's largest lizard is the mighty Komodo dragon (bottom) which lives on the islands of Indonesia. Its bite is ferocious and can take down prey as large as a water buffalo. If the bite doesn't finish the victim off, the lethal, venomous **saliva** it injects will.

Lace monitors (left) from Australia are equally vicious. Their speed, power and sharp teeth can rip through flesh and bone.

TRUE OR FALSE?

The Gila monster (below) from North America is a lizard so toxic that its breath can kill you if you get too close. **True or False?**

FALSE! The Gila monster is venomous and has a fearsome reputation, but stories of toxic breath and spitting venom are just myths. In fact it is rarely a threat to humans.

Komodo dragons tear off large chunks of flesh and eat them whole.

FIERCE CROCODILES

A crocodile is one of the few animals on Earth that will deliberately set out to hunt, kill and eat a human. These enormous beasts are also extremely fast and powerful, which means they can catch and devour any prey they like.

A crocodile's eyes and ears are on the top of their head allowing them to hide in the water.

CRUSHING CROCS

The saltwater crocodile is the largest **reptile** in the world, growing up to seven metres in length. Found in South-east Asia and Australia, this monster croc dines on monkeys, sharks and buffalo, as well as humans. Its powerful jaws, lined with over 60 sharp teeth, can snap shut with massive **force**.

AMAZING FACT
The death roll

A crocodile's 'death roll' is one of the most powerful killing moves on the planet. Few creatures will survive it. The croc clamps its jaws onto the prey, drags it underwater and rolls over again and again in a manic spin until the victim has drowned. This rips limbs and chunks of flesh from the victim, which the crocodile then swallows whole!

A crocodile's attack is sudden and devastating.

TRUE OR FALSE?

The crocodile has the strongest bite in the animal kingdom. **True or False?**

TRUE! The force of its bite is over 12 times more powerful than a great white shark's!

The Nile crocodile (above) is found in the marshes, rivers and lakes of Africa. Like other crocs it lies in wait, hidden almost completely under the water. Just its eyes and nostrils are **visible** so it can see and breathe. Then – in the blink of an eye – it lunges out of the water to grab, drown and eat its prey.

ALLIGATOR ATTACKS

You can tell the difference between an alligator (below) and a crocodile by looking at the head. An alligator's nose is rounder and its teeth do not stick out when its jaws are shut. But alligators can be just as deadly as crocodiles. People foolish enough to swim in the rivers of the south-eastern United States can be ripped apart by the American alligator.

ALLIGATOR JOKE

Q How many legs has an alligator got?

A It depends how far he has got with eating his dinner!

GIANT BEASTS

Some animals are so huge that once they start **charging** they can cause total destruction. It is important not to **startle** these beasts because that is when they become seriously aggressive.

Elephants are not meat-eaters, yet they are one of the most dangerous animals in the world. Hundreds of people are killed each year by the African elephant, the largest and heaviest land animal on Earth. Weighing the same as a double-decker bus, it will crush any threat that stands in its way.

ELEPHANT JOKES

Q What's the best way to see a charging **herd** of elephants?

A On television!

Q Why are elephants wrinkled?

A Have you ever tried to iron one?

ON THE CHARGE

Rhinos don't like humans very much. It's no wonder as we have hunted these animals for thousands of years. If they get mad, these strong, heavy beasts can charge at you at speeds of up to 50 kph (30 mph). Rhinos will trample you or use their horns to gore you to death.

African buffalos are even more terrifying. To defend themselves they charge in huge herds at great speed. Their large and deadly horns are joined together by a rock-hard plate on their foreheads. African buffalos kill more people in Africa than lions.

ANGRY HIPPOS

The hippopotamus is one of the most aggressive creatures in the world and one of the deadliest in Africa, killing more people than lions or crocodiles. You might think that they are fat and slow animals that laze around in the water and mud. But hippos can turn into savage beasts. Armed with tusks as long as swords they can turn boats over and deal a killer bite. On land they are fast runners and can crush victims like a heavy tank.

AMAZING FACT
Leader of the pack

Male buffalos fight each other with their horns to decide who should be in charge of the herd. Usually the male buffalo with the thickest and sharpest horns wins. The victorious male must see off any threats to the herd. He leads the way and races at the front of the herd when it **stampedes** towards a victim.

TRUE OR FALSE?

Hippos were brought to ancient Rome to fight gladiators. **True or False?**

TRUE! It was done to celebrate Rome's 1,000-year anniversary in 248BCE.

THE BIG CATS

Members of the big cat family are among the most feared predators on Earth. Lions, tigers and leopards are incredibly powerful and quick for their size. They do not usually attack humans, but if they are hungry – and you are the only meat around – they will hunt you for food.

AMAZING FACT
The tiger's roar

The roar of the tiger must be the most frightening sound in nature. To be up close to it would be deafening – the roar is 25 times noisier than a petrol lawnmower! The roar is so loud and deep it can be heard over three kilometres away.

The teeth of a tiger are perfect for snapping a victim's neck and tearing up flesh.

TIGERS ON THE HUNT

The tiger is the largest and strongest of all the big cats. This magnificent hunter measures up to three metres in length and over a metre high. It uses its strong senses of smell, sight and hearing to find its prey and can jump high, climb trees and swim fast. The tiger's strength can hold down and drag huge prey, from buffalo to bears. It grips on to its victim with its jaws and kills it by biting its throat or breaking its neck.

TRUE OR FALSE?

Old lions and tigers with missing teeth are the most dangerous to humans.
True or False?

TRUE! They struggle to catch and eat their normal prey so they will attack humans instead.

IN FOR THE KILL

It is not just power and speed that make the big cats expert hunters. Some use deadly **stealth**. The tiger's black stripes blend in with the shadows of the forest so its victims cannot see it until it is too late. The jaguar (left) of South America uses the same tactic. In perfect camouflage, it creeps slowly through the forest… and then suddenly it leaps on to its prey. Its teeth are so strong that it can kill animals by biting through their skulls.

Leopards (below) are super strong. They can drag prey three times their own body weight up into a tree to stop other animals reaching it.

The cheetah is the fastest predator on land, chasing down prey at a speed of over 100 kph (60 mph). You are better off staring this cat in the eye to scare it off, rather than running away.

Pumas (right), also known as cougars or mountain lions, live in North and South America. They are awesome sprinters and jumpers. A puma can leap 12 metres and clear 3-metre fences with a fully grown deer in its jaws!

Puma attacks have increased in recent years as more people enter their territory.

BIG CAT JOKE

Q Which cat can jump higher than a tree?

A Any cat can jump higher than a tree. Trees can't jump!

HUNTING IN PACKS

Lions are the only big cats to live in groups. These top predators chase down their victims as a team, giving their prey little chance to escape. A lion group is called a pride and can include up to 30 lions. Male lions have a **mane** to help them look bigger and more fierce. They rarely hunt but they are still deadly. Their job is to keep the pride safe.

Female lions, called lionesses, are quicker and do the hunting for the pride. On the hunt, several lionesses circle a herd of prey such as buffalo or zebra. Then they close in and make a final quick dash, leaping on to their chosen victim (above).

AMAZING FACT
Top dogs

The African hunting dog works in packs of up to 60. These savage dogs carry on chasing their prey for hours until it is totally exhausted. Their incredible stamina means 80 per cent of their hunts result in a kill. This makes them one of Africa's most effective predators. Lions on the other hand make short bursts of speed and often give up. Only 30 per cent of lion hunts end in a kill.

WILD WOLVES

Grey wolves from Asia and North America are the largest members of the dog family. Working in teams, they can bring down prey much larger than themselves, such as **moose** and **bison**. The wolves spread out when chasing their prey to block off any escape routes. As they get closer they bite chunks of flesh from the victim's legs and rear, causing a massive loss of blood. This slows the prey down and the wolves then go in for the kill by biting the animal's throat. The excited wolves then rip and tug the dead animal's body in all directions, eating large chunks of flesh as quickly as they can.

A pack of grey wolves feed on their kill.

HYENAS

Spotted hyenas from Africa are ferocious animals for their size. They can drive leopards and lions away from their kills and have been known to bring down a hippopotamus. Packs of hyenas run into a herd and select an animal to attack. They then chase their prey for several kilometres at speeds up to 60 kph (37 mph). Once the catch is made the hyenas eat the victim alive. No waste is left behind. With their powerful jaws they can crush up bones, which they digest completely. At night, hyenas can become man-eaters. They prey on people who sleep outdoors in camps.

BRUTAL BEARS

Big bears are aggressive, dangerous beasts. In fact they are the biggest land **carnivores** in the world. They can swim, run fast, climb trees, and they eat everything from berries to humans.

Grizzly bears in North America will usually only attack humans if they feel their cubs are under threat. But if a bear is feeling hungry it is wise to stay far away. Grizzly bears are powerful. One swipe of their paws can knock you down and do some serious damage. Many hikers in forests have been **mauled** to death. The American black bear is smaller than the grizzly bear but still dangerous. They are experts at sniffing out food. Hungry bears sometimes wander into towns tearing down doors, raiding houses and causing havoc.

Grizzly bears are very aggressive when they are defending themselves.

AMAZING FACT
Surviving a bear fight

If you meet a bear in the woods don't stare it in the eye or you might make it mad. Stay calm and move slowly away without making a noise. If the bear does charge at you, stand your ground and it may think twice about attacking. Don't run away or climb a tree – it might chase you and tear you to pieces. If the worst happens and you get into a fight with a grizzly bear, pretend you are dead and protect your neck – you might just get out alive!

Black bears are smaller than grizzlies so it is possible to fight them back. Punching a black bear in the nose or poking it in the eye with a stick might scare it away. If you are heading into areas where bears live, always take friends with you. Bears are less likely to attack a group. And keep your food well sealed so that bears are not attracted to you.

BEAR JOKE

Q What is a bear's favourite day of the week?

A Chewsday!

THE BIGGEST BEAR

The polar bear is the largest bear, weighing nearly four times more than a lion. Polar bears dine on seals and sometimes whales. They are amazing and brutal hunters, using their strength, sharp claws and deadly teeth to rip apart their victims. Food is in short supply on the Arctic ice, so they would definitely see a human as lunch!

Polar bears are huge, weighing up to 700 kilograms and measuring three metres long.

TRUE OR FALSE?

While on the hunt, polar bears cover their black noses with their paws to camouflage themselves against the snow. **True or False?**

FALSE! – probably. Early Arctic explorers reported seeing this but there is no evidence to say that it is true.

ASIAN ATTACKERS

In Asia, moon bears (left) and sloth bears are very aggressive towards humans. Both have powerful upper bodies for climbing trees and massive paws. In fierce attacks they stand up on their hind legs and slash at a person's face with their claws. Then they knock their victims down and chew them to pieces with their sharp teeth.

A great white shark launches itself out of the water off the coast of south Australia.

HUNGRY SHARKS

Sharks are the most fearsome hunters in the sea. These ferocious predators can sense tiny traces of blood in the water from several kilometres away. However, out of the 360 species of shark, only four of them will eat humans.

GREAT WHITE SHARKS

The most famous and terrifying shark is the great white. Great white sharks are found in all of the world's oceans. They are built for speeding after prey with their massive **streamlined** bodies that can grow over six metres long. They surprise their victims by striking from below and pulling them under water with their jaws. The shark then thrashes its head from side to side using its razor-sharp teeth to saw off huge chunks of flesh.

TRUE OR FALSE?

Great white sharks are the most dangerous man-eaters on the planet. **True or False?**

FALSE! They make very few attacks on humans. Since 1990 there have been just over 140 attacks. Many attacks happen because the shark has mistaken a human for normal prey such as seals. After one bite, great white sharks will often swim away. Humans are just too bony for their taste.

SHARK JOKE

Q What do you get from an angry shark?

A As far away as possible!

TIGERS, BULLS AND WHITETIPS

Tiger sharks (right) get their name from the stripes running down the sides of their bodies. They have a massive head filled with deadly teeth that can slice through turtle shell and even chomp through metal. Tiger sharks often visit shallow **reefs** and harbours where they sometimes prey on humans.

AMATING FACT
The rubbish bin with fins

It's no wonder tiger sharks will eat humans because they are not fussy. Lumps of wood, bags of potatoes, car tyres and even a suit of armour have been found inside a tiger shark's stomach!

Bull sharks

Bull sharks live in warm waters across the world. They are fierce and can travel up rivers far inland. This, and their unpredictable nature, make them very dangerous. Horses, humans and even hippos have been victims of their vicious attacks. The bull shark circles its prey and then charges at it, like a bull, before biting it. Out of all the sharks it has the most destructive bite.

Oceanic whitetip

Oceanic whitetips are different. They live far out in the middle of the ocean, but they still love to eat humans. Shipwreck and air crash victims make a perfect dinner for these open-ocean monsters.

LETHAL FISH

Swimmers should be beware. Hidden under the water lie some terrifying and deadly fish.

SEABED SHOCKER

The most venomous fish in the world, the stonefish, lives along the coasts of the Indian and Pacific Oceans. This grumpy looking beast lies among the rocks and does not like to be disturbed. Sticking up from its back is a row of 13 sharp **dorsal** spines. If a swimmer steps on it, the spines shoot deadly venom into the victim. The pain is terrible and the victim can lose their leg and even their life. Stonefish blend perfectly into the seabed. The danger is you won't see it until it is too late.

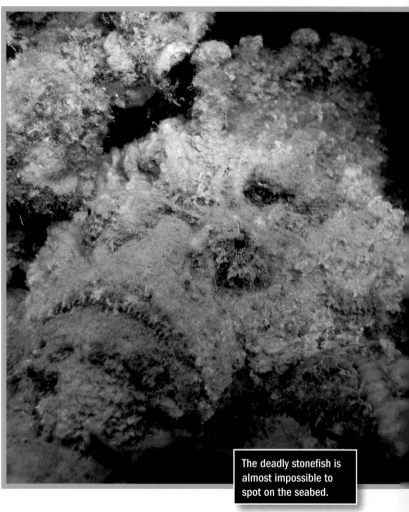

The deadly stonefish is almost impossible to spot on the seabed.

MEAT-EATING FISH

Red-bellied piranhas (left) have fearsome appetites. They live in the rivers and streams of the South American rainforest. Stay out of the water in these places because attacks on swimmers can be brutal. With their razor-sharp teeth they hunt in **shoals**, making mincemeat of their prey.

TRUE OR FALSE?

Red-bellied piranhas can tear a human body to shreds in seconds. **True or False?**

FALSE! – not that quickly. But they could eat a human alive, furiously stripping the flesh from their victim's bones.

RAYS AND PUFFERS

Stingrays (right) are large, flat fish that have a lethal form of self-defence. On the stingray's tail are large, venomous spikes called barbs. If attacked it can suddenly whip its tail around, spiking its victim. This can kill a human if the barb pierces a vital **organ** such as the heart.

Electric eel

Pufferfish (below) are covered in small spines. These strange creatures can gulp in water and blow themselves up like a balloon to warn off predators. Even if a pufferfish is eaten, the predator is likely to die, because the pufferfish's insides are extremely toxic. Dishes made from pufferfish are served in some restaurants and are popular in Japan. But if the chef doesn't prepare the food properly, the dish is deadly. Would you risk ordering it?

AMERICAN FACT
AMAZING FACT
Electric eels

Electric eels are weird, monster fish that can grow to the size of a large dog. The eel's organs can produce an **electric charge** of over 500 volts, enough to kill a human at close range. After stunning its prey, it sucks it into its mouth. The eel's body is covered in slimy skin to protect it from its own electricity.

The insides of a spiny pufferfish are toxic and dangerous to eat.

TINY BUT DEADLY

Size isn't everything. The most dangerous creature in the world is just a centimetre long and weighs less than a gram.

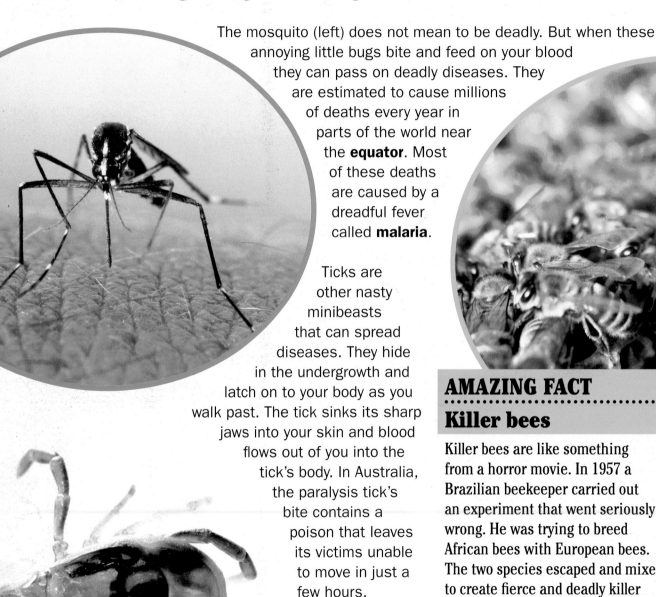

The mosquito (left) does not mean to be deadly. But when these annoying little bugs bite and feed on your blood they can pass on deadly diseases. They are estimated to cause millions of deaths every year in parts of the world near the **equator**. Most of these deaths are caused by a dreadful fever called **malaria**.

Ticks are other nasty minibeasts that can spread diseases. They hide in the undergrowth and latch on to your body as you walk past. The tick sinks its sharp jaws into your skin and blood flows out of you into the tick's body. In Australia, the paralysis tick's bite contains a poison that leaves its victims unable to move in just a few hours.

Paralysis tick

AMAZING FACT
Killer bees

Killer bees are like something from a horror movie. In 1957 a Brazilian beekeeper carried out an experiment that went seriously wrong. He was trying to breed African bees with European bees. The two species escaped and mixed to create fierce and deadly killer bees. These bees have now spread across much of North and South America. They attack in huge swarms and will chase their victims for miles!

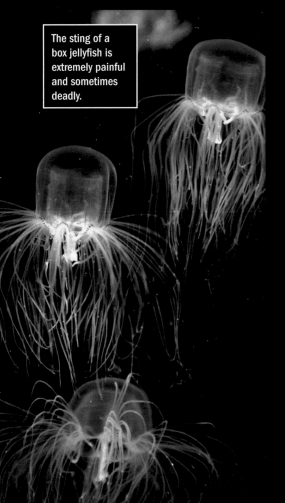

The sting of a box jellyfish is extremely painful and sometimes deadly.

TERROR UNDER THE WATER

Tiny but deadly creatures lurk under the water too. The blue-ringed octopus (right) is found in rock pools off the coast of Australia. It is not much bigger than a golf ball but it is one of the most venomous creatures on the planet. The scary thing is you won't know you have been bitten. The bite is painless but you could be dead in a few minutes.

The box jellyfish (left) is a swimmer's nightmare. **Tentacles** covered in lethal, stinging cells trail from its body. These shoot darts of venom into anyone who brushes past. The fast-acting venom causes shock and heart failure and victims often drown.

AMAZING FACT
Shell-shocked

Cone shells are beautiful, small sea snails that live on coral reefs in the Indian and Pacific Oceans. Picking one up could be deadly. The snail shoots venom into its victims with a harpoon-like tooth. Once dead it sucks the prey into its shell to digest. The venom is strong enough to kill a human and there is no known antivenom.

QUIZ

How much have you learned about dangerous animals from reading this book? Here is a quiz to test your memory.

1. What type of creature is a wolverine?

2. How does a green anaconda kill and eat its prey?

3. Which is the fastest moving snake in the world?
   a) king cobra
   b) black mamba
   c) death adder

4. How does the Goliath birdeater tarantula attack humans?

5. Which is the most toxic scorpion on the planet?

6. How did poison dart frogs get their name?

7. Which is the world's largest lizard?
   a) Gila monster
   b) lace monitor
   c) Komodo dragon

8. How does a crocodile kill its victims?

9. Which animal kills the most people in Africa?
   a) hippo
   b) lion
   c) crocodile

10. How do a tiger's stripes help it to hunt?

11. How do African hunting dogs catch their prey?

12. What should you do if a grizzly bear attacks?

13. Which man-eating shark can be found in rivers?

14. Which is the most venomous fish in the world?
   a) stonefish
   b) pufferfish
   c) stingray

15. Why are mosquitoes so deadly?

AMAGING FACT
Death tolls

Snakes	kill over 50,000 humans each year
Scorpions	over 5,000
Hippos	nearly 3,000
Crocodiles	over 2,000
Elephants	over 500
Lions	over 200
Sharks	10–20
Tigers	5–15
Bears	5–10

GLOSSARY

antivenom a medicine used to treat the poisoning caused by an animal venom

arachnid an animal with four pairs of legs and a body divided into two segments, such as a spider, scorpion or tick

bison a humpbacked ox with a shaggy mane and a massive head with curved horns

bloodstream the blood that runs through the body of a person or animal

cancer a disease that spreads throughout the body causing damage to cells

carnivore an animal that feeds on flesh

charge rush forward in attack

coil wind around something in a series of rings

digest break down food in the stomach into substances that can be used by the body

dorsal relating to the back of an animal

electric charge the quantity of electricity in a substance

equator the imaginary line around the centre of the Earth that divides the north from the south

force the strength of a movement

herd a large group of hoofed animals that live together

hibernate spend the winter in a deep sleep

infect to fill with germs that cause disease

inject to force a fluid into a body part by piercing the skin

malaria a deadly disease that causes fevers, chills and sweating

mane a growth of long hair on the neck of a lion or other animal

mating coming together for breeding

mauled beaten up or torn savagely

moose a large deer

organ a part of the body that performs a vital function such as the heart or eye

predator an animal that hunts and kills other animals

prey 1) hunt and kill for food 2) an animal hunted and killed by another for food

rabies a deadly disease that attacks the brain, which can be passed on by the bite of an animal such as a dog or bat

rainforest thick forest found in warm areas that have heavy rainfall

reef a ridge of rock, coral or sand just above or below the surface of the sea

reptile a cold-blooded animal, such as a snake, lizard or crocodile

saliva a watery liquid in the mouth that helps animals to swallow and chew food

shoal a large number of fish swimming together

stampede charge forward at speed in a large group

startle to cause sudden shock or alarm

stealth quiet or secret movement

streamlined shaped so that it can cut through the air or water with little resistance

tarantula a very large, hairy spider

tentacles thin arms used by sea creatures for feeling, grasping or moving

territory an area that an animal lives in and defends

toxic poisonous

venom a poisonous fluid produced by animals, such as snakes and scorpions, and injected into their victims' bodies by biting or stinging

visible in view

WANT TO KNOW MORE?

Here are some places where you can find out a lot more about dangerous animals:

WEBSITES

www.animaldanger.com
Find out about the most dangerous animals in each of the world's continents.

http://animals.nationalgeographic.com/animals/big-cats-initiative/
This site contains lots of information about big cats.

www.kidzone.ws/lw/snakes/facts.htm
For a closer look at snakes.

http://www.spidersworlds.com
All about all kinds of spiders.

www.bbc.co.uk/nature/life/Shark
Contains useful information and fascinating videos about sharks.

BOOKS

Animal Attack series, Alex Woolf,
(Franklin Watts, 2014)

Animal Planet: World's Most Dangerous Animals, Darren Vincenzo, (Zenescope, 2012)

Deadly Animals: Ultimate Top Tens. Meet the World's Most Dangerous Creatures, Kim Bryan, (Tick Tock Books, 2012)

Deadly!: The Truth About the Most Dangerous Creatures on Earth, Nicola Davies, (Walker, 2013)

The Most Dangerous, Terri Fields,
(Sylvan Dell Publishing, 2012)

Website disclaimer:
Note to parents and teachers: Every effort has been made by the Publishers to ensure that these websites are suitable for children, that they are of the highest educational value, and that they contain no inappropriate or offensive material. However, because of the nature of the Internet, it is impossible to guarantee that the contents of these sites will not be altered. We strongly advise that Internet access is supervised by a responsible adult.

INDEX